Revolution
— poems of the necessary uprising

by Wendy Mulhern

To every rising heart, and each one that desires to rise

Contents

Introduction:

We are living in a world of fearsome challenges: the rampant greed and thoughtlessness of the powers controlling policy and resources, the meaningless consumption of the life energies of the planet — the biosphere, the waters, the hours of people's lives. We find the tools we thought we had are useless — our voice in government wholly bought out, our voice in public debate mostly marginalized by the corporate interests which own the media.

There are some positive developments coming to light, however. We hear of a dawning awareness that the decisions taken do not represent our choice. We hear of people withdrawing consent from the status quo. And we are starting to grasp that there is power in our individual life choices. These poems arose from my desire, my need, to have a life that makes a difference — a life, in fact, that brings on a revolution. I hope this volume, voicing my rising empowerment, will in turn empower others to bring about the necessary changes in how we live in the world.

You Must Not Hide Your Power

No, you must not hide your power
Nor stuff it in a shell of smallness
in some attempt at bland conformity;
Must not succumb to thoughts that say
To cloak your power
would make you more like others,
More acceptable, more lovable,
Deserving of more care —
That, to fit in, you must be small like them.

No one is small!
And you must not be fooled
by shells that make them seem so
or games that shells may seem to play.

If you stand up
And breathe into the depth
of your own power
You will awaken
a rush of recognition
And hear the ripping
of all the shells of smallness
Cracking open, falling off from all the others
Who each have found their power
And now step free.

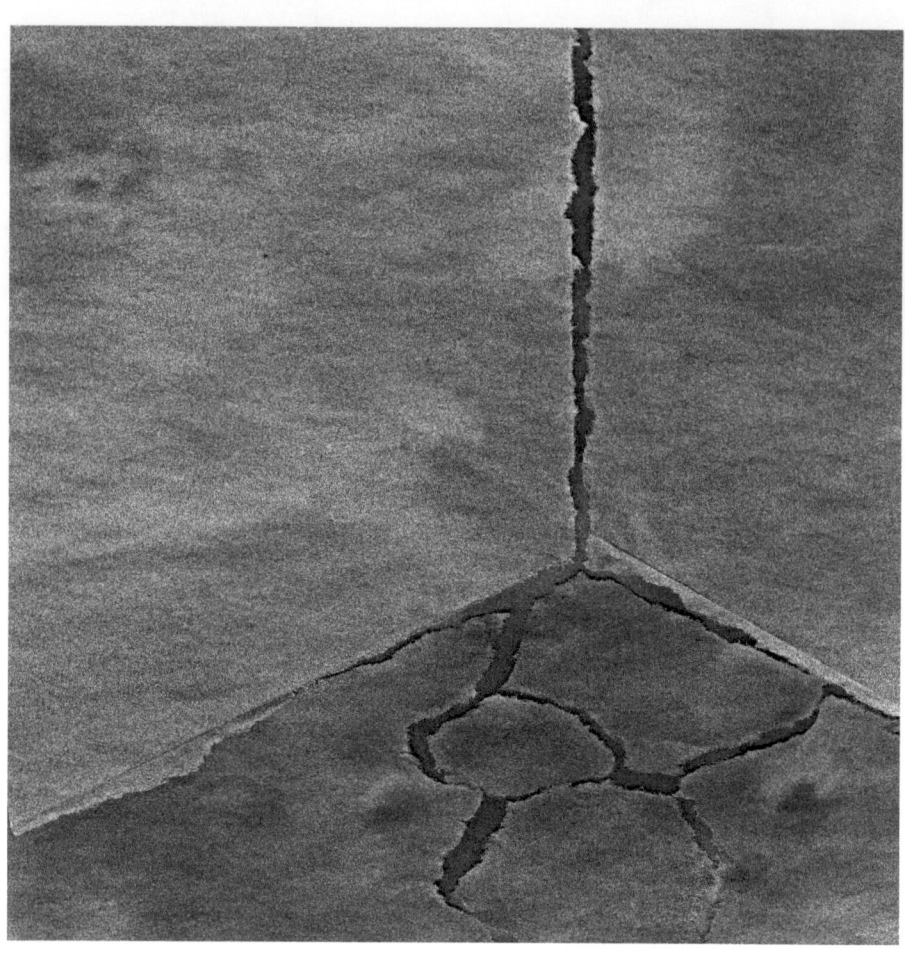

Revolution

The revolution will not happen by itself.
I can't turn over for another hour's sleep,
Then see it like late morning's sun,
so many hours risen . . .

The revolution will not happen
from my smugness
where I pretend I've worked out
all my issues
and can simply wait . . .

The revolution needs
my deep insistence, daily
on the laws which cause my brightness
and every dawn
and refusing to again be duped
by any story casting life as barren.

The revolution takes knowing
You are needed
I am needed
Each one needed, uniquely
Swelling in the firm, insistent way of seeds
Whose self-unfoldment cracks the rocks
Each tiny one performing
Its own miracle of growing
So the revolution comes.

Critical Mass

It seems to still take a certain mass
or else I am critical
of myself
and my efforts
and my contribution
and I hold back
stay in the shadows
don't speak out, don't dance
I've heard tell that the instinct
is ancient, animal tribal,
a necessary coordination
safeguarding collective survival —
the strength and shared warmth of a herd
within which one can feel secure
But I
my voice so thoroughly revoked
by lack of others
feel more like I have failed myself
have lacked the courage of convictions
let my message fall to silence
before I would be seen to stand alone.

Manifesto

We've been trained
these many years
not to ask for much —
That we don't deserve
that we have no right to expect
daily abundance and joy
That to receive it
we must earn it
through great toil and sacrifice

Worse than that
we're taught that it's OK
to wish to have, to win,
to rape, to dominate,
to blindly flail, mindlessly mouth
the words of hate —
That if we strive to beat each other
we'll be great

So it is
that the first revolution
is within
To see we have the right
to be at peace
to have a world designed to bless
where each of us can know
that we deserve
to have our lives be cherished, recognized as gifts
not weighed for what they pay, and then perhaps
begrudgingly allowed

And as we give this to each other
we will learn
how it is done
how we can sculpt a greater vision
so we know what's to be won
and then we'll march unhesitating
shining whole before we're through
for the sake of billions waiting
standing strong because we're true.

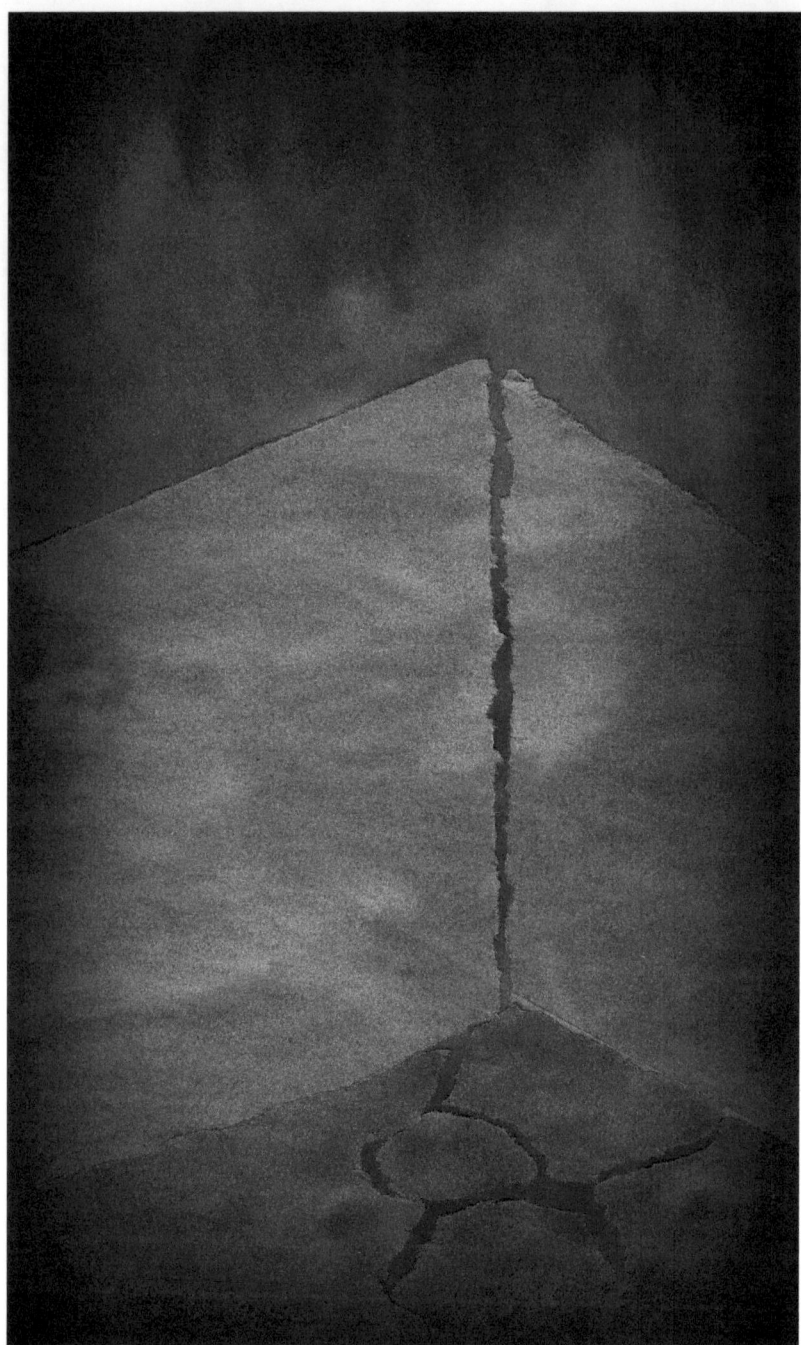

Isaiah 52:3

ye have sold yourselves for nought. . . .

ah, verily
we have sold ourselves for a bargain:

community
       for low prices at Costco

neighborhood
       for hundreds of channels on Comcast

livelihood
       for cheap wares from China . . .

sackcloth and ashes!
       for we have not been conquered
       no brave stand against the cannons
       no soul bracing acts of raw courage
       no
we just sat here.

ye have sold yourselves for nought
       (wait, this has happened before —)
ye have sold yourselves for nought,
and ye shall be redeemed without money.

we shall not be bought!
we shall be redeemed!
with that which can't be bought
but can be given.

No

This may be the game
but it is not mine
This may be the game
but it is not life

So much complexity
So many things to study
So many permutations
to distract us, keep us tangled

The hand you're dealt, we're told,
You have to play
You may be lucky, privileged or poor
Or maybe you are brilliant but disturbed
Addicted, disadvantaged, or a rising star

It only makes a little difference, though:
As long as we've consented to be playing
There isn't very far that we can go
We all remain imprisoned in the game.

Today I mouth my infant words
of no
No, I won't play; no, this is not my game
I won't define you by your cards or course
I won't pick up the dice of shame and blame
I won't be cowed by game-incurred alarms
or things the game insists I have to prove
I won't let any game-based definition
distract me from my purpose and my love.

Fight Mode

I am called to fight
Roused to fierce defense
Shaking the bland shroud
That duped me for so long
That said, you are free — see?
You're free to choose
And you (collectively) have chosen
To step on the heads of others
while running this ugly treadmill
You have chosen
To buy what you want
For the low cost of your souls
And let the land be raped
Just so you wouldn't know.
No! I did not choose this
And no I do not want this
And no I will not let you take
My supple soul.
So I stand
Centered, wary
Charged by a line of power
Pulling an ancient strength
Down through the lines of life
Star-started DNA
Holding me steady
Source-aligned thunder
Clearly aimed, ready
I have been wakened to see through the sham
I will defend us with all that I am.

More than Survival

It may be
that love is so potent
we can survive
on just a tiny bit
We may think
if we can have
enough love to survive
we should be happy
We should then be willing
to slave through our days
herded and cordoned
cogs in massive machinations
of meaningless things
We may have been told
we don't deserve more
That if we're lucky we'll have
a few loves in our life
which we can string as charms
along our chains
and limp from year to year
between the times our loves have shined
But look what we can have!

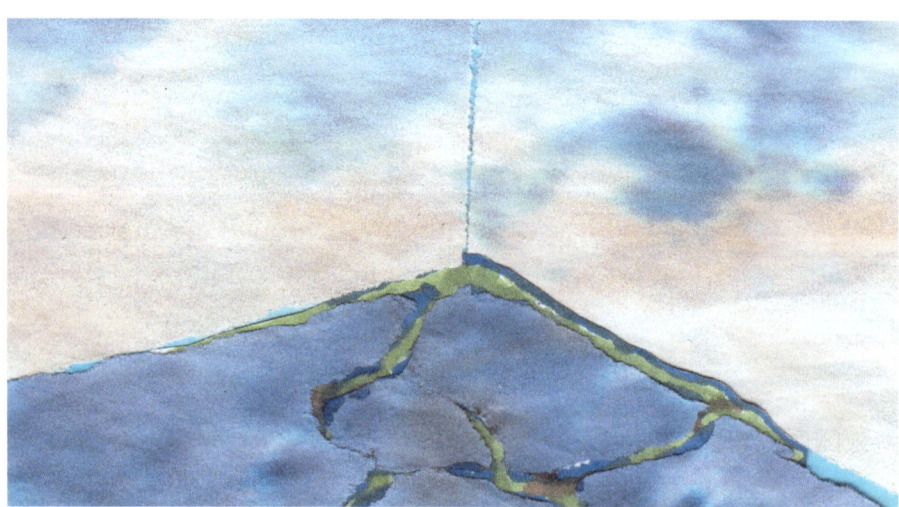

Look how love dissolves
all the expectations
Look how it fills us
and teaches us
We need more than survival
We need this love
that has filled us once
to now be there constantly
We need it to spread
like a flash flood
till it redefines everything
All landscapes now filled
with its presence.

Monday, Downtown

Oh, humanity!
Working at your tired charades
Moving through so many empty boxes
Desiccated corridors
Courses without meaning

Look how amazing you are!
Look how, even when the rules are cast
to close out any purpose, light, or joy
You still find ways to shine:
Through this skewed account of life
your light slips through the chinks
and though at times refracted
blazes forth
Makes us maybe take a while to notice
all the places where it is suppressed
Just think: if we were free
what brilliance we would show

It is our destiny
We will prevail
We will shine clear
We'll banish all the false demands
The failed array of hoops, constrictive bands
Deny the faulty purposes
that disappointed us
Swing free
on the strength of our unstoppable
creative rush!

In Tune

To be in tune
is such a natural thing
though unacknowledged
in our benighted sphere
A thing that babies know at birth
and try with some success at first
to teach their parents

Why do we then fall into such confusion
Thinking that we're born without a clue
and must be plied with tedious instruction
before there's anything we know that we can do?

It opens up a yawning gap
that stretches over many weary, lonely years
of seeking satisfaction in the proffered tasks
expected failure deepening our fears
When what we really wanted
is so close to us, so simple
To listen once again to infant wisdom
To find the ancient science of connection
Ride on the waves
that make us move as one.

Nourishment

In the face of everything
we've been fed
Empty, deadening, toxic
I still affirm
We can know what feeds us

Despite the false choices
with which we're inundated day by day
the cheap vulgarization of our triggers
the sea of trash that can't be thrown away
I still affirm
We can know what we want

And though the words of love
have been so thoroughly misused
applied to tiny wicked shards
that cut us as they shine
made to divide us
where love most wishes to unite
We still will find
Inside, we know what love is
And it outweighs all the lies

And everyone who's tasted love must give it
And in the giving it will grow
Till more and more of us can truly live it
And every need will be well fed
in its bright glow.

Perspective

The truth endures in geologic time
Where stones, in their inexorable leisure
Form and re-form,
Sifting, vaulting, melting,
Crystalize in metamorphic treasure
And all the impositions on our days
The despotism, lies, and power plays
Are nothing — have no weight
And own no time
And can't establish anything that stays.
What though their dark impress has pulsed
through generations,
dampening their light?
The voice of truth is not reversed
and so it dawns
on every sight.
These dreams will prove
ephemeral, irrelevant
Our waking rocklike, pure
eternal
Heaven-sent.

The Language of Touch

The language of touch
Is as broad, and as nuanced
As any language
And it can be learned
And passed from one to another
Like any language
And like many native languages
It has been forbidden
It has been almost lost
But it can be reclaimed
Pieced together and reconstructed
From the snatches of what we remember
What some gifted few
Embody
It can spread like oil
It can multiply
Till every body knows
How to speak it
And it can sing
In rich and glorious harmony
Shared, rising, rebellious
Overthrowing the long-enforced silence
That kept us boxed off from each other
We will sing this language
Of touch
Until everyone hears it
And finds the way home.

Deliverance Prayer

Bring my soul up out of Egypt
Walk me step by patient step
out of the patterns that enslave me
Release me from the lockstep
that doesn't look
that is afraid to seek the kinship of a smile

Teach me to spin out on the leaf edge
of the wind
and twirl into the knowing
of the infinite variety —
Intricacies which Life has ever blessed

Let me no longer follow
the commands that run them over
that allow us three or four straight norms at best
Unclamp my feet from marching
Free my toes
to find the subtle footholds
midst the wildness of the river

Free the rivers, too
and let us all please tumble brightly
down the perfect, wild, unchanneled
course that we were born for
Let us know each other
deeply, truly, freely

Bring my soul up out of Egypt
That I may worship
My Good.

Idols

Winds of Spirit
Sweep my thought
It's time to cast out idols
Those who ask for time
Those who ask for blood
Those who ask for tiresome daily ritual
Who say they have the power
to save my sorry life
or, if I fail to worship,
occasion my demise

But they know nothing, and their mouths can't speak
The life they offer is anemic, weak
And Spirit shows me, right here, what I am
Exposing all their noxious threats as sham

I will not worship
the god of appearances
I will not worship
the god of social norms
I will not worship
the god of shopping bargains
I will not worship
the god of health concerns

Winds of Spirit, sweep my soul
I am made to worship
what is true and whole
That frames the space for all that's free and wild
And holds us each as Life's untrammeled child.

Manifesto II: Tipping

The old story must
fall away like a husk
for it is too dry
to sustain the living —
those who now stride
into their own

Since there is no place for them
in the old story —
No job, no niche, not even
one small joy to suck on,
They will turn
and find their sustenance within
and with each other

And those who managed the old story
may try, once again, to recalibrate —
Give them just enough juice
so they will stay
But it's too late
The load has tipped:
With a grand whoosh
all the piled up lies
will slide into oblivion
And we will put forth
our new green.

Infinite Comfort

What rescues you
when you are smothered under
the sense of being thought of as a number? —
the numbing nothingness of being counted,
accounted for,
packaged and dispatched,
your measure taken,
assessed, dismissed
and so forsaken?

Any act of life can rescue you
and anyone or any living thing can do it
The scent of petals, kissed by warming wind,
A smile unweighed, uncalculated, treasured,
Or seeing someone needs you as a friend,
A gift of time untallied and unmeasured —
Whatever focuses on what is infinite
will make a place for you
and bring you into it.

Ashes, Ashes

Reason unravels
Reasons unravel
Following the rules —
staying within the lines —
are shown to hold no more safety
Anyone can fall . . .

When the perimeter permitted is too small
to let us range
And it grows tighter
narrowing our path until we pace in figure eights
And we are running them like caged cats
in frenzy, beating out our necessary rhythm
in a permission-starved place
where there's no room for us
There will be breakages
and the rules won't keep us safe.
Ashes! Ashes!

So it will continue
till one by one
we withdraw consent
to any rules that hem in our compassion
and rationalization that results in isolation
and any, all partitions based on fear
We can't be safe until we come together
in the place that holds us all,
that holds us tender
Refusing scorn, refusing condemnation.

(The only way to bring someone to justice
is to be just
to banish from within the urge to hate
No lashing out in anger can release us
But grief's collective wail
experienced in union
may let us see each other,
bring us home.)

Howling

Go ahead
Stomp if you need to
Raise your fist at the sky
and scream
Swear, howl, wail
Your thoughts aren't holding up the world
Your actions, however desperate
can't damn you
The Love that holds you
is well able to sustain the world
and you
through this storm
whether it's your storm
or all the world kicked up around you
whether you feel you have been bad
or feel you have been wronged
It doesn't matter
You can rest
The Principle that turns the worlds
will keep on turning
Your drooping hopes will raise their heads
towards morning.

Liberation

Nothing stops you.
But what wrestling will it take
To break free of every hook in thought
that snags against your fabric
so you're caught
And makes you think you have no choice at all?

Nothing stops you.
But what words can overcome
the song of chains
you've heard so long you find its rattle soothing
Because (you think) it shows you where you are?

Nothing stops you.
In this moment you can rise to grasp
the vastness of your being
and the endless sky,
The power coiled within
that now can launch you free
to spin your dance across the deep expanse of space
Always supported in your native grace.

Imposter

It's not your voice, I told him,
that censures you, that censures me
that seeks to keep us hemmed in
on a narrow path between our fears
with needs that go unclaimed, unmet
through weary, empty years
separated from each other
so we never feel
the grand connection that could comfort us
and flawlessly reveal
the glorious fireworks of our being
all the color, all the light
continuous igniting
of the flame that pulses bright
to mark the vastness of the universe
in which we freely roam
which is defined by us
and is our rightful home
Your voice, I told him,
won't consign our souls to hell
It knows what's true about you
and it knows it well.

Who Rules You?

If God is a tyrant
It doesn't matter who rules you —
which voices, external or internal
bear down on you
bend you to their yoke
You have no hope for freedom anyway
Only the hope of bargaining
for some marginally less paltry
slice of life

But if there is freedom anywhere
If there is fulfillment
If there is any love, any bright joy
Then something must be holding up the ceiling
of the sky
Some law must make provision
for dynamic lift

If God were a tyrant
There would be no point in life at all
But Life rises
irrepressible
and joy is real, and comes unbidden
Flashes of brilliant day
take us by surprise
proving
God is not a tyrant
and you can have
everything you love.

Salvation

"And I will rebuke the devourer for your sakes"

As the devourer chomps
more and more bites
from our collective day
And there are ever fewer places
its great maw has not marred
And as we see the things we hoped for swallowed —
their pieces spit back on the putrid heap —
And feel the seemingly inexorable churning
of sacrificial goods conveyed to feed the beast
What can deliver us?

What can deliver us?
Not only from the looming shadow —
swift encroaching hopelessness, despair —
But also from the soporific tendency
to sink in hooded apathy
or hide in empty revelry
To close our eyes as if we didn't care. . .

Truth can deliver us
The truth of each one's heart's desire
must reaffirm its presence
The law of motivations
must ascend in every life
Till all that is perverted falls
and only what is true remains.

"Then will I also confess unto thee
that thine own right hand can save thee."
— And each yearning heart
that answers its own call
will help to realign our lives
and save us all.

The Meaning of Hope

For those of you who never found
in the box of proffered choices
anything that fed your soul
Who turned back sadly
While others raced towards goals
for which you had no interest

For those of you who never thought it fair
to have to settle for the duties of the day
Who couldn't bring yourselves to care
for all the regulations of the game
Though voices of authority intoned
"Grow up, assume your role, and play"

Take heart, for that same discontent
Reveals another world beyond the game
A place where all your heart's desires are met
Where what you are receives its right acclaim

What you must give may not be found in stores
May not be priced and parceled, stamped and screened
But it is real, and when you bring it forth
It starts to map the world for which we dream
Each of your earnest hopes affirms the presence
Of your beloved, unarguable essence.

Wild

It doesn't matter
when and how it started —
those first moments of the inner wildness,
The ones that stirred you
till you had to notice.
Once you noticed
you had to pay attention.
Once you paid attention
it had to grow
and will,
till suddenly it overthrows the systems,
colossal though they are,
and comprehensive, and entrenched,
that claimed to rule you for so very long.
Those systems have no power
against inexorable wildness
that always follows
the laws of your true essence.
You will never again be tame
and you will know
that being good
has nothing to do with following someone else's rules
and everything to do with being you.

Reclamation

After the voice of scorn was banished
Other voices began to rise
tentative at first,
but gaining strength from each other
The voice of wonder
The voice of "of course!
You have a right to joy;
Of course goodness is the organizing principle!"
The voice of liberation
The voice of exaltation
The voice of a continual elation
Realizing every silenced hope
could claim its place
and start to sing again.

Homing

The water is homing
Carving deltas in the sand
Delta for change
though this is timeless
Water homing
A grand joining
from every place where it had seeped
at high tide
Water flowing
in zigzag patterns of the moment
through the sand
Pooling in our footprints
Dissolving them, but halted
for a time
in the impressions

Water like multitudes, molecules
Each called alone
Moving together as one
Water like
us claiming our freedom
through the simple act
of moving as we are called.

Ancient Ways

In my tribe
the way it was
before the ancient ways were lost
to history, and to other tools
with which we've been subverted,

In my tribe
each infant soul
was braided with such care
into the stream of all of us
that none was ever dropped or lost
and as it grew
each one learned its vital, pulsing rhythm
and its needed place
how to move strongly in the power of its knowing
how to contribute, how to own its name

So we were all
united with the magic
and we strode along the elemental forces
and our hands knew how to bring
each fine idea to fruition
and our feet knew how to run the ancient courses

As they will again, as we remember
all the pathways of our common dreams
how to mirror forth our inner splendor
and braid ourselves together in the stream.

Remembering

We walk almost in trance
Remembering
Doing things no one has taught us
Doing them because we must —
Some ancient edict
has brought us to this point
Insistent hunger drives us to the place
where we may find ourselves together
learning grace

Slowly, we pick up and wear the wisdom
Older than the schools
and the long, loud rush of words
and the frantic reasoning
intoned over and over
The words of those who would impose
a logic to their will
and make us think we need to do
the things that scatter, kill
us off, to cull the ones
who for a time can do the bidding
of a voice that doesn't care.

But we return
Some of us, at first
Then a few more
We come in ones and twos
But we are many
And listening within
Each of us knows
this thing we need to do
So we unite
First join hands
Then learn to breathe together
Then learn to hold the space for one another,
To shine the light that magnifies each person's gift
That brings us into peace and closes up the rift
Till we can weave our separate music into one voice
To reconstruct our primal song, and so rejoice.

Deep thanks to Shannon Noel for catalyzing the theme for the artwork, and for empowering me as a visual artist. I am in awe of her gift. Thanks to Scot Robinson for helpful consultation on the arc of the poems and images in this collection, and on many particulars of the layout. Thanks to Heather Mulhern for technical support and ongoing encouragement. And special thanks to Edward Mulhern, my co-revolutionary and continuing support.

About these poems

In the fall of 2010 I began the practice of writing a poem
a day. At first I was writing sonnets, and the topic wasn't
highly important to me. It was enough to work on the
form of the verse — the meter, the rhyme, the structure.
But soon I found that, somewhere within the discipline,
poignant themes would emerge — things I hadn't known
I felt or knew. And it became important to me — more
important than the form — that my poems capture this
honest essence, speak truly about whatever was most
salient in my day. Sometimes it has been an idea, an
image, a metaphor; sometimes the coloring cast by an
emotion over an everyday event. Sometimes the weather,
sometimes its internal equivalent.

Over the course of weeks and months, certain themes
emerged in my poems. One of them I labeled Revolution.
These poems chronicled my own uprising against
forces that have enslaved me, and my claiming of a new
liberation — one I claimed with surprise, not having
known, before, that such a state was possible. And I
felt the rising desire to have everyone participate in this
liberation, to have it impact not just individual lives but
also the way we live collectively — a desire which also
found its way into these poems.

This volume is a collection of the best of my poems on this theme, arranged in an arc to show the progression of liberation, and illustrated to show the inexorable power of the necessary uprising. In publishing this book, I add my voice to many who are speaking out for our right to be free, our right to thrive.

— *Wendy Mulhern, 2013*

About the author

 Wendy Mulhern is a poet, a spiritual seeker, a dancer. She lives in Seattle with her husband, her father-in-law, and her two almost grown children, when they are not away at school.

She writes a poem a day (almost) and publishes her poems at wendymulhernpoetry.blogspot.com. For news of her print publications, see wendymulhern.com.

Also by Wendy Mulhern:

Capture Rapture — *notes from the romance adventure.*

Capture Rapture is about romance — all facets of it — from the initial attraction through all the uncertainties and questions, and including both the joy of union and the necessary regrouping when things don't work out as hoped. Through all the aspects of romance, it provides spiritual resources that lead to the calm of love.

Infinite Permission — *a healing journey home*

Infinite Permission will take you along a path of liberation —

liberation from constricting concepts of body image, identity, and purpose to a fuller range of movement and a deeper sense of spiritual wholeness. Wendy Mulhern's tender poetry finds a synergistic accompaniment in Mellissae Lucia's luminous art.